TABLE OF CONTENT

TABLE OF CONTENT 2

1. MOCHA JAVA SMOOTHIE 4
2. MUSHROOM AND OLIVE SKILLET FRITTATA 4
3. PEANUT BUTTER WAFFLES 5
4. POACHED EGG OVER GRITS 6
5. PUMPKIN MUFFINS 7
6. PUMPKIN PANCAKES 8
7. PUMPKIN PIE SMOOTHIE 9
8. PUMPKIN SPICE FRENCH TOAST 11
9. SPINACH CHEESE SQUARES 12
10. SPINACH, FETA, AND TOMATO EGG MUFFINS 13
11. COCONUT STRAWBERRY SCONES 14
12. STRAWBERRY KIWI SMOOTHIE RECIPE 15
13. STRAWBERRY RICOTTA CREPES 16
14. SUMMER BREAKFAST PARFAIT 17
15. SUNRISE SMOOTHIE 18
16. TEX MEX BREAKFAST CASSEROLE 19
17. HOW TO TURN PANCAKE MIX INTO WAFFLE MIX 20
18. VANILLA MANGO SMOOTHIE 21
19. GRANOLA & YOGURT BREAKFAST POPSICLES 21
20. ALMOND CHEESECAKE BARS 22
21. COCONUT ALMOND BISCOTTI 23
22. ALMOND FLOUR CRACKERS (1 BOWL!) 24
23. STICKY ASIAN CHICKEN WINGS 26
24. KETO BLT CUCUMBER STACKS 27
25. BANANA NUT COOKIES 28
26. BUFFALO CHICKEN BITES (BONELESS BUFFALO WINGS) 29
27. CANDIED PECANS 30
28. VANILLA MANGO SMOOTHIE 31
29. CHEDDAR CRISPS 32
30. CHEESE AND ONION DIP 33

- **31. CHEESY PITA CRISPS** 34
- **32. CHEWY GRANOLA BARS** 35
- **33. CHILI LIME TORTILLA CHIPS** 36
- **34. CHOCOLATE CHIP BLONDIES** 37
- **35. APPLE CHIPS** 38
- **36. APPLE CINNAMON POPCORN** 39
- **37. ALMOND CRANBERRY GRANOLA BARS** 40
- **38. CREAMY SPINACH CRAB DIP** 41
- **39. CHEDDAR CHEESE PUFFS** 42
- **40. APPLE FRIES** 44
- **41. DOUBLE CHOCOLATE BISCOTTI** 45
- **42. FIG BARS** 47
- **43. THE BEST LEMON BARS** 48
- **44. FREEZER FUDGE** 49

1. MOCHA JAVA SMOOTHIE

Ingredients

- 1 tbsp sugar
  2 rounded tsp instant espresso, or 2 shots of espresso
  2 tsp unsweetened natural cocoa powder
  ¼ cup of boiling water
  2 cups of nonfat milk
  2 ripe bananas, peel off, slice into chunks, refrigerated
  1 cup of ice

Directions

1. Mix the sugar, cocoa powder, and instant espresso, if using, in a small bowl. Stir until dissolved after adding the boiling water. (If use ordinary espresso, thoroughly incorporate the sugar and chocolate into the coffee.)

2. Bananas, milk, ice, and the coffee mixture should all be mixd in a blender. Blend on high until completely smooth.

2. MUSHROOM AND OLIVE SKILLET FRITTATA

Prep Time: 5 minutes

Cook Time: 15 minutes

Servings: 1

Ingredients

- 2 tbsp Ava Jane's Kitchen Avocado Oil

- 1/2 cup of thinly split mushrooms

- 1/2 tsp dried thyme

- 3 eggs beaten

- 1/4 cup of shredded mozzarella cheese
- 2-3 sun dried tomatoes split
- 1/4 cup of olives any kind, pitted and split
- Fresh chop up parsley for serving

Instructions

1. A nonstick skillet is warmed up over medium-high heat. Add the mushrooms, thyme, and avocado oil. Use a slotted spoon to remove from pan after cooking until thoroughly browned.

2. When the edges are set, add the eggs and cook for one minute. Lift the edges with caution and allow the liquid to run beneath them. Reduce the heat to low and sprinkle the cheese on top. Cook the eggs thoroughly and melt the cheese in the pan for 2 to 3 minutes under cover. Add sun-dried tomatoes, mushrooms, and olives as garnish. Before serving, top with black pepper, Colima Sea Salt, and parsley.

3. Nutrition

4. The following nutritional breakdown is given in calories: 594kcal; 6g of carbohydrates; 25g of protein; 53g of fat; 12g of saturated fat; 7g of polyunsaturated fat; 31g of monounsaturated fat; 1g of trans fat; 513mg of cholesterol; 908mg of sodium; 468mg of potassium; 2g of fiber; 2g of sugar; and 1131IU of vitamin A; 7mg of vitamin C; 247mg of calcium

3. PEANUT BUTTER WAFFLES

Ingredients

- 1 3/4 cups of all-purpose flour (spooned and leveled)
- 2 tbsp sugar
- 2 tsp baking powder
- 1 tsp baking soda
- 1/2 tsp coarse salt
- 1/4 cup of (1/2 stick) unsalted butter, melted, + more for brushing waffle iron
- 6 tbsp creamy peanut butter
- 2 cups of buttermilk

- 2 large eggs
- 3 bananas, split, for serving
- 3/4 cup of pure maple syrup, for serving

Directions

1. Waffle iron should be hot and the oven should be preheated to 275 degrees; lay a wire rack on a baking sheet with a rim and put it in the oven. Mix the flour, sugar, baking soda, baking powder, and salt in a big bowl. Butter and peanut butter should be blended for one minute, until creamy. Eggs and buttermilk should be blended for a minute to mix. Just until batter is mixed, add buttermilk mixture to flour mixture.

2. Pour 1/2 to 3/4 cup of batter into waffle iron, leaving a 1/2-inch border on all sides, and brush with butter. Close the iron and cook the waffles for 2 to 4 minutes, or until golden brown. Repeat with the remaining batter after transferring the waffles to the oven's warming rack. Serve with maple syrup and bananas.

4. POACHED EGG OVER GRITS

Ingredients

- 2 tsp white vinegar
- 1 large egg
- Creamy Calcium Grits
- Coarse salt and freshly ground pepper

Directions

1. 3 inches of water should be added to a large saucepan or high-sided skillet. Using a high heat, bring to a boil. Add vinegar and stir. In a little, shallow bowl or cup of, crack an egg. Increase simmer to a high setting. Just bring the egg-filled bowl up to the simmering water's edge. Pour the egg quickly into the bubbling water. If necessary, a spoon can be used to keep egg whites together. Simmer for about 4 minutes, or until yolk is just set.

2. With the help of a slotted spoon, remove the poached egg and quickly drain it on paper towels. Over the creamy calcium grits, place an egg. Serve right away after adding salt and pepper as need.

5. PUMPKIN MUFFINS

Prep:15 mins

Cook:15 mins

Ingredients

- 225g plain flour
- 2 tsp baking powder
- 1 tbsp ground cinnamon (or 2 tsp pumpkin spice)
- 100g caster sugar
- 50g soft light brown sugar
- 200g pumpkin purée (from a can or homemade – see 'goes well with' below)
- 2 large eggs
- 125g slightly salted butter, melted

Method

1. STEP 1: Preheating the oven to 200°C/180°F fan/gas 6. Put muffin liners in a 12-hole muffin pan. In a sizable basin, mix the flour, baking powder, cinnamon, and both sugars. Rub any brown sugar clumps between your fingers to break them up.

2. STEP 2 Mix the eggs and purée in a jug and then stir them into the dry ingredients together with the melted butter. Using an electric hand whisk, mix ingredients for 1-2 minutes.

3. STEP 3 Bake for 15 minutes, or until the top is risen and brown and a spear inserted comes out clean. Lift up onto a wire rack to finish cooling. When stored in an airtight container, it will last three days.

6. PUMPKIN PANCAKES

Prep Time: 10 mins

Cook Time: 15 mins

Total Time: 25 mins

Servings: 6

Ingredients

- 1 ½ cups of milk
- 1 cup of pumpkin puree
- 1 large egg
- 2 tbsp vegetable oil
- 2 tbsp vinegar
- 2 cups of all-purpose flour
- 3 tbsp brown sugar
- 2 tsp baking powder
- 1 tsp baking soda
- 1 tsp ground allspice
- 1 tsp ground cinnamon

- ½ tsp ground ginger
- ½ tsp salt
- cooking spray

Directions

1. In a big basin, thoroughly mix the milk, pumpkin, egg, oil, and vinegar.
2. In a another bowl, stir together the flour, brown sugar, baking soda, allspice, cinnamon, and ginger. Add the mixture to the pumpkin, and stir just until incorporated.
3. Cooking spray a griddle or frying pan; heat over medium-high heat.
4. For every pancake, pour 3 to 4 tbsp of batter onto the heated griddle and flatten the batter just a little with a spoon.
5. Cook for 2 minutes or until tiny bubbles start to emerge.
6. About two more minutes after flipping, heat until golden brown.
7. Use the leftover batter to repeat.

7. PUMPKIN PIE SMOOTHIE

PREP TIME 10 MINUTES

TOTAL TIME 10 MINUTES

SERVES 1

Ingredients

- 1 refrigerated banana
- ½ cup of plain or vanilla yogurt
- 1/2 cup of pumpkin puree
- 1/2 cup of unsweetened almond milk
- 1 tbsp almond or pecan butter
- 1 tsp vanilla extract
- 1/2 tsp ground cinnamon
- pinch every of nutmeg, ginger & allspice

Instructions

1. **Blend all ingredients in a blender until they are completely smooth. Serves 1. Feel free to substitute pumpkin pie spice for the cinnamon, ginger, and nutmeg in this recipe.**
2. **Use your preferred dairy-free yogurt to make it dairy-free.**
3. **For more advice and information, read the entire post.**

Nutrition

Servings: 1 serving

Serving size: 1 smoothie

Calories: 320kcal

Fat: 10.4g

Saturated fat: 0.6g

Carbohydrates: 38.5g

Fiber: 8.8g

Sugar: 22.4g

Protein: 17.1g

8. PUMPKIN SPICE FRENCH TOAST

prep: 15 MINUTES

cook: 10 MINUTES

total: 25 MINUTES

INGREDIENTS

- 4 large eggs
- 1 cup of whole milk
- ¾ cup of canned pumpkin puree
- 1 ½ tsp pumpkin pie spice
- 1 tsp vanilla extract
- ¼ tsp kosher salt
- 1 loaf brioche or Challah bread, slice into 1-inch thick slices
- ¼ cup of unsalted butter, separated
- ¼ cup of maple syrup
- 1 tbsp confectioners' sugar

INSTRUCTIONS

1. Eggs, milk, pumpkin pie spice, vanilla, salt, and pumpkin puree should all be mixd in a big bowl. Bread slices should be dipped into the egg mixture one at a time and left to soak for at least 10 seconds.
2. Over medium heat, melt 1 1/2 tsp of butter in a big skillet.

3. Working in batches, add bread slices to the skillet and cook for 2-3 minutes on every side, or until both sides are uniformly golden brown. With the remaining bread and butter, repeat.

4. Serve right away with maple syrup and, if preferred, confectioners' sugar as a garnish.

9. SPINACH CHEESE SQUARES

Prep Time: 10 mins

Cook Time: 35 mins

Additional Time: 45 mins

Total Time: 1 hrs 30 mins

Servings: 11

Ingredients

- 2 tbsp butter
- 3 eggs
- 1 cup of all-purpose flour
- 1 cup of milk
- 1 tsp baking powder
- 1 pound shredded Cheddar cheese
- 2 (10 ounce) packages refrigerated chop up spinach
- 1 tbsp chop up onion

Directions

1. Set the oven to 350 degrees Fahrenheit (175 degrees C).

2. Melt butter in an oven by pouring it into a 9x13-inch baking dish. After three minutes, when the butter has melted, remove the dish.

3. In a sizable mixing bowl, beat the eggs. Add the baking powder, milk, and flour and stir to incorporate. Add the cheese, onion, and spinach. Fill the baking dish with the mixture and butter it.

4. For 35 minutes, bake in the preheated oven. Once cool, slice into bite-sized squares after cooling for 45 minutes.

10. SPINACH, FETA, AND TOMATO EGG MUFFINS

Prep time: 10 mins

Cook time: 20 mins

Total time: 30 mins

Serves: 12

Ingredients

- 10 eggs
- baby spinach
- grape tomatoes (halved or quartered)
- crumbled feta cheese
- 1/3 cup of milk
- salt and pepper

Instructions

1. Turn on the 375 degree oven.
2. Apply nonstick spray to muffin pan.
3. Every cup of should contain tomatoes, baby spinach leaves, and crumbled feta.

4. Salt and pepper are whisked in with the milk and eggs.

5. Pour every cup of with the egg mixture.

6. 20 to 25 minutes of baking.

11. COCONUT STRAWBERRY SCONES

Prep Time:10 minutes

Cook Time:15 minutes

Total Time:25 minutes

Ingredients

- 320 gr (2 1/2 cups of) Plain Flour
- 50 gr (1/4 cup of) Brown Sugar
- 50 gr (1/2 cup of) Shredded Coconut
- 1 1/2 teasp. Baking Powder
- 1 pinch Salt
- 50 gr (1/4 cup of) Unsalted Butter
- 2 Eggs
- 180 ml (3/4 cups of) Coconut Cream
- 200 gr (7 oz) Strawberries

Instructions

1. While preparing the batter, slice your strawberries into little pieces and lay them in the freezer to solidify (see note 1).

2. Mix the flour, brown sugar, shredded coconut, baking soda, and salt in a sizable bowl.

3. When the butter is added, use a pastry cutter to chop it in until it is crumbly (see note 2)

4. Use your fingertips to incorporate the eggs, coconut cream, and dry ingredients into a homogeneous dough in a separate bowl. Avoid working the dough too much.

5. Quickly knead the dough after adding the refrigerated strawberries. In order to prevent crushing the strawberries, try not to press down too firmly.

6. While your oven is preheating, chill the dough.

7. Set your oven to 180 degrees.

8. Flour your work surface and scones dough slightly, then roll every piece into a thick circle that is about 2 cm high.

9. Slice the scones using a cookie cutter into the desired size and shape, then arrange them on a baking sheet covered with parchment paper. Make sure there is enough room between every scone since they will rise.

10. Before eating, let them cool on a cooling rack after baking for 15 minutes (see note 3).

11. Serve with cream and strawberry jam.

12. STRAWBERRY KIWI SMOOTHIE RECIPE

Prep Time 5 minutes

Total Time 5 minutes

Servings 2 servings

Ingredients

- 2 cups of refrigerated strawberries thawed for 5 minutes
- 2 medium-sized kiwis peel off and slice in half
- ½ cup of milk unsweetened*
- ¼ cup of yogurt plain*
- 1-2 Tbsp. sweetener non-compulsory

Instructions

1. Blend all ingredients in a blender like a Nutribullet or Vitamin. Place the refrigerated items further away from the blade and the softer ingredients closer to it.

2. Blend until creamy and smooth for 1 to 2 minutes.

3. Straws are non-compulsory, as are diced strawberries and kiwis. Enjoy!

13. STRAWBERRY RICOTTA CREPES

Total: 1 hr 35 min

Active: 55 min

Ingredients

- Deselect All
- Crepes Batter:
- 1 cup of all-purpose flour
- 2 tbsp sugar
- 1/4 tsp kosher salt
- 1 cup of whole milk
- 1/4 cup of water
- 3 large eggs
- 3 tbsp unsalted butter, melted and cooled
- Filling:
- 2 cups of split strawberries
- 5 tbsp honey
- 1/2 cup of fresh ricotta, drained overnight
- 2 tbsp chop up fresh mint

- Zest of 1 lemon
- Nonstick cooking spray
- aConfectioners' sugar, for dusting

Directions

1. In a medium basin, mix the flour, sugar, and salt to make the crepe batter. In a blender, mix the milk, water, eggs, and melted butter. Until smooth, blend. Mixture of flour is added. Just till smooth, scraping down the blender's carafe's sides as necessary. If you have the time, let the batter rest in the fridge for 30 minutes.

2. Split strawberries and 2 tbsp of honey should be mixd in a medium bowl for the filling. If you have the time, refrigerated for 30 minutes.

3. With a wooden spoon, mix the fresh ricotta that has been drained with the remaining 3 tbsp of honey, the mint, and the lemon zest in a medium bowl. Beat until smooth and light.

4. A big nonstick saute pan or crepe pan should be heated over medium heat. Apply cooking spray liberally. About 2 ounces of the crepe batter should be poured into the pan's center and swirled. A spatula should be used to flip the food once the center starts to firm. Cooking time for every side should be 2 minutes. Use the leftover crepe batter to repeat this (it will make 8 to 10 crepes).

5. Roll up the crepes after stuffing them with the ricotta filling. Strawberries should be spread over the crepes. Sprinkle some confectioners' sugar on.

14. SUMMER BREAKFAST PARFAIT

INGREDIENTS

- 1 cup of Vermont Morning Multi-Grain Hot Cereal - dry, not cooked
- 1 cup of non-fat plain yogurt
- 1/4 apple, cored, chop up
- 1/2 banana, split
- 12 grapes, slice in half (or not)

- Try your other favorite fruits, fresh or dried.
- Milk (non-compulsory)

PREPARATION

1. Mix the dry cereal grains with the yogurt, cover and refrigerated overnight. (An option is to add dried fruit at this point so they soak up the moisture from the yogurt as well as the grains.) In the morning, scoop out your serving size and top with your favorite split / chop up fresh fruit. Adding a bit of milk will make it smoother. For plain yogurt, you may want to sweeten it with a bit of honey or sugar-free sweetener. I love the interplay of tart and sweet and don't add anything but friut!

15. SUNRISE SMOOTHIE

Total: 5 min

Prep: 5 min

Ingredients

- Deselect All
- 1 cup of chop up ripe strawberries (5 large strawberries)
- 1 cup of chop up seeded watermelon
- 1 cup of chop up fresh peach
- 1 cup of raspberry sorbet
- 1/4 cup of freshly squeezed orange juice

Directions

2. Using a blender, purée the strawberries, watermelon, peach, sorbet, and orange juice until they are creamy and smooth. If you'd prefer it to be a little less thick, add additional orange juice. Serve immediately with straws in large glasses.

16. TEX MEX BREAKFAST CASSEROLE

Prep: 20 mins

Cook: 1 hr

Total: 1 hr 20 mins

Ingredients

- 14.5 ounce can diced potatoes, or 1 3/4 cups of diced cooked potatoes
- 2 links cooked chorizo sausage, diced (3 1/2 ounces) I used Goya
- 2 cans, 4.5 ounces chop up green chiles, undrained
- 2 cups of shredded Colby-Monterey Jack cheese
- 12 large eggs
- 1/2 cup of chop up scallions
- 1/2 tsp seasoned salt such as Adobo
- 1 jalapeno, split thin
- 4 ounces 1 small haas avocado, split
- 1 cup of chunky mild salsa

Instructions

3. Cooking spray should be used to coat a 3-qt (9" x 13") oblong glass Pyrex baking dish.
4. The potatoes should be put in the baking pan. Add 1 cup of the cheese, the chorizo, and the green chilies on top.
5. Whisk eggs, scallions, and salt in a medium bowl until thoroughly mixd. Give the potato mixture a pour.
6. If preparing the night before, cover with a lid and place in the refrigerator.

7. Remove from the refrigerator and allow it to come to room temperature before baking.

8. Oven temperature set to 325 °F.

9. Until a knife inserted close to the center comes out clean, bake uncovered for 55 to 60 minutes.

10. Slices of jalapeno and the remaining cup of cheese should be added after taking it out of the oven.

11. 2 more minutes of baking is required to melt the cheese. Slice the dish into 10 squares, then top with salsa and avocado to serve.

17. HOW TO TURN PANCAKE MIX INTO WAFFLE MIX

Prep: 1 minute

Cook: 5 minutes

Total: 6 minutes

Ingredients

- 1 cup of favorite pancake dry mix (Try our delicious and healthy oatmeal pancake mix!)
- 2 tbsp cooking oil (i.e. melted coconut oil, avocado oil, etc.)
- The liquid or other ingredients listed on your pancake mix box/recipe (i.e. water, milk, eggs)

Instructions

1. Two tsp of oil should be added to every cup of dry pancake mix. Next, mix all of the extra liquids and ingredients mentioned in the recipe or on the package.

2. Just enough waffle batter should be added to cover the waffle iron, and the waffles should be done after 3 minutes. (Check the directions for your waffle maker.)

18. VANILLA MANGO SMOOTHIE

Prep Time: 5 minutes

Cook Time: 0 minutes

Total Time: 5 minutes

INGREDIENTS

- 1 cup of refrigerated mango
- 1 refrigerated banana
- 1/2 cup of unsweetened vanilla almond milk*
- 1/2 tsp vanilla extract
- 1 scoop vanilla protein powder (I use North Cost Naturals Vanilla Whey
- non-compulsory: 1 cup of baby spinach

INSTRUCTIONS

1. Blend every item in the blender until it is smooth.
2. Drink right away.
3. Use any non-dairy milk you like. In this smoothie, I adore using unsweetened coconut milk!

19. GRANOLA & YOGURT BREAKFAST POPSICLES

Active: 20 mins

Total: 8 hrs 20 mins

Servings: 6

Ingredients

- 1 ¼ cups of low-fat plain yogurt
- 1 ½ cups of chop up fresh berries (strawberries, blueberries, raspberries and/or blackberries)
- 4 tsp pure maple syrup, separated
- 1 tsp vanilla extract
- 6 tbsp granola, large chunks crumbled

Directions

1. In a medium bowl, mix yogurt, berries, 2 tsp maple syrup, and vanilla. In six 3-ounce popsicle molds, divide the mixture. In a separate bowl, mix the remaining 2 tsp of maple syrup with the granola. Add 1 spoonful of the granola mixture to the top of every popsicle. Place popsicle sticks inside and freeze for the night.

20. ALMOND CHEESECAKE BARS

Prep: 20 min. Bake: 35 min. + cooling

Ingredients

- 2 cups of all-purpose flour
- 1 cup of butter, softened

- 1/2 cup of confectioners' sugar
- filling:
- 1 package (8 ounces) cream cheese, softened
- 1/2 cup of sugar
- 1 tsp almond extract
- 2 large eggs, room temperature
- frosting:
- 1-1/2 cups of confectioners' sugar
- 1/4 cup of butter, softened
- 1 tsp almond extract
- 4 to 5 tsp 2% milk

Directions

2. the oven to 350 degrees. Press the mixture of flour, butter, and confectioners' sugar into the bottom of a 13 x 9-inch baking pan that has been oiled. Bake for 20 to 25 minutes, until golden brown.
3. Cream cheese, sugar, and extract should be smoothed out in a small bowl. Just until mixed, add the eggs and beat on low speed. over the crust. Bake for 15-20 minutes, or until center is almost set. on a wire rack to cool.
4. To make the frosting, mix all ingredients in a bowl and beat until smooth. Place in the fridge to store.

21. COCONUT ALMOND BISCOTTI

Ingredients

- Top of Form
- 2 1/2 cups of all-purpose flour
- 1 1/3 cups of unsweetened shredded coconut

- 3/4 cup of split almonds
- 2/3 cup of sugar
- 2 tsp baking powder
- 1/2 tsp salt
- 1 extra-large egg at room temperature
- 1 extra-large egg white at room temperature
- 4 ounces (8 tbsp, 1 stick) light butter, melted
- 1 tsp vanilla
- Bottom of Form

Directions

1. Oven rack in the center; heat to 350 degrees. Use parchment paper or a nonstick liner to line a baking pan.
2. In a sizable basin, mix the flour, sugar, baking soda, salt, coconut, and almonds. Mix thoroughly with an electric mixer set on low speed.
3. In a medium bowl, briskly whisk the egg, egg white, butter, and vanilla. Add to the dry ingredients and mix on low speed.
4. Slice the dough in half, equally. With lightly dusted hands, form every piece of dough into an 8 x 2 3/4-inch loaf. On the prepared baking sheet, space the loaves 3 inches apart.
5. Until brown and firm, bake loaves for 26 to 28 minutes. Cool for ten minutes on a wire rack. Slice every loaf into 1/2-inch-thick slices using a serrated knife. Slices should be placed slice side down on a baking pan. Bake for 20 minutes, or until brown and firm. Complete cooling on a wire rack.

22. ALMOND FLOUR CRACKERS (1 BOWL!)

PREP TIME 5 minutes

COOK TIME 20 minutes

TOTAL TIME 25 minutes

Ingredients

- 3/4 cup of almond flour (we prefer Wellbee's)
- 2/3 cup of tapioca flour (also called tapioca starch)
- 1 ½ tsp flaxseed meal (ground flax seeds)
- 1/2 tsp sea salt
- 1/8 tsp baking soda
- 1/8 tsp garlic powder (non-compulsory)
- 2 Tbsp olive oil
- 3/4 tsp maple syrup
- 2 ½ Tbsp water

Instructions

1. Put a big baking sheet in the oven and preheat it to 325 degrees F (162 degrees C).
2. Almond flour, tapioca flour, flaxseed meal, salt, baking soda, and garlic powder should all be mixd in a medium mixing basin (non-compulsory). Mix thoroughly, breaking up any clumps as you go.
3. The olive oil and maple syrup should be poured into the center of the dry ingredients after creating a well. To evenly incorporate the oil and maple syrup into the flour mixture, use a fork or clean hands. Add the water now and stir. The dough in the bowl can be kneaded with your hands to create a cohesive dough. Add a tsp at a time of extra water if it is too dry.
4. Your work area should be covered with a piece of parchment paper before you add the dough. A second piece of parchment should be placed on top of the dough after rough rectangle-shaping it. The dough should be rolled out to about 1/16 inch thick. To slice the crackers into roughly 1 12-inch squares, use a pizza cutter or knife. Transfer the crackers to the baking sheet that has been prepared with parchment paper using a metal spatula or knife.
5. Bake the crackers until brown, about 17 to 22 minutes. The length of the bake depends on how thick the crackers are. Watch them closely since they start to quickly turn brown near the finish. Before consuming, let the pan to cool completely.

6. Remaining crackers can be kept in the fridge or freezer for up to a month, or at room temperature for up to 5 days in an airtight container.

23. STICKY ASIAN CHICKEN WINGS

PREP TIME10 minutes

COOK TIME20 minutes

TOTAL TIME30 minutes

Ingredients

- 1 lb. (0.4 kg) chicken wingettes and drumettes
- salt
- ground black pepper
- cooking spray
- 1 cloves garlic, chop up
- 1/2- inch (1 cm) piece ginger, peel off and chop up
- 2 1/2 tbsp honey
- 1 1/2 tbsp soy sauce
- 1/2 tbsp garlic chili sauce
- 1/2 tbsp apple cider vinegar or 1 tsp chop up roasted peanut
- 1 tsp chop up cilantro leaves

Instructions

1. The chicken wings should be washed and dried with paper towels. Add some salt and freshly ground black pepper as need. Place the chicken on a baking sheet covered in aluminum foil and spray it

lightly with cooking spray. Turn the chicken over and broil the opposite side for 3-5 minutes after broiling the first side for 12 to 15 minutes, or until well browned and slightly scorched.

2. Garlic, ginger, honey, soy sauce, garlic chili sauce, and vinegar should all be mixd in a small sauce pan. Simmer until thickened and just barely sticky on low heat. Toss the chicken wings with the sauce to thoroughly coat them. Place the chicken wings on a serving plate and garnish with the cilantro and peanuts. Serve right away.

24. KETO BLT CUCUMBER STACKS

Ingredients

- Cucumber, Raw, With Peel
- 2-¼ ounce
- Cream Cheese
- 4 ounce
- Bacon Bits, Pork
- 1-½ tbsp
- Cheddar Cheese
- 2 tbsp, shredded
- Grape Tomato
- 4 grape
- Lettuce
- ¼ ounce
- Recipe Steps
- steps 3
- 12 min

Instructions

1. Slice a cucumber into 9, 1/4-inch-thick slices. Before adding toppings, dry them between paper towels.

2. Before using a fork to mix bacon bits and shredded cheddar, make sure your cream cheese is melted and at room temperature.

3. Every slice of cucumber should have roughly 12 TB of cream cheese filling on top of it. Place the diced tomatoes and lightly shredded lettuce on top of the cucumber slices. To ensure that the ingredients stick, gently press them into the cream cheese.

25. BANANA NUT COOKIES

Ready In: 22mins

INGREDIENTS

- 1/2cup of unsalted butter, room temperature
- 1cup of sugar
- 1egg, room temperature
- 1cup of mashed banana (about 2 1/2 large bananas)
- 1tsp baking soda
- 2cups of flour
- 1pinch salt
- 1/2tsp ground cinnamon
- 1/2tsp ground nutmeg

- 1/2tsp ground cloves
- 1cup of chop up nuts (pick your favorite or even add chocolate chips)

DIRECTIONS

1. Oven: 350 degrees Fahrenheit Cream the butter and sugar until it is frothy and light. Beat the mixture after adding the egg until it is frothy and light.

2. Baking soda and mashed bananas should be mixd in a bowl. Give it two minutes to sit. The acid in the bananas will react with the baking soda, giving the cookies their lift and rise.

3. Mix the butter mixture with the banana mixture. Sift the flour, salt, and spices together, then stir them briefly into the butter and banana combination.

4. If using, fold the chop up pecans or chocolate chips into the batter. Drop dollops onto a baking sheet covered with parchment paper. 11 to 13 minutes in the oven, or until well browned. Place wire racks to cool.

5. roughly 30 cookies are produced.

26. BUFFALO CHICKEN BITES (BONELESS BUFFALO WINGS)

Prep Time: 5 mins

Cook Time: 25 mins

Total Time: 30 mins

Servings : 8

Ingredients

- 2 lb boneless skinless chicken breast, patted dry and diced into 2" pieces

- ½ c cornstarch, or arrowroot powder for paleo
- 2 tsp sea or kosher salt
- 1 tsp cracked black pepper
- 1 tsp onion powder
- 1 tsp garlic powder
- ½ tsp paprika
- 2 tbsp olive oil, or avocado oil for paleo
- ½ c Frank's RedHot
- ½ c Texas Pete Original Hot Sauce, or your favorite hot sauce – see suggestions in post
- 2 tbsp butter

Instructions

1. In a sizable mixing bowl, mix the cornstarch, salt, pepper, paprika, onion powder, and garlic powder. Stir everything together completely.
2. When the chicken is all coated, add it to the cornstarch mixture and toss.
3. A 12" nonstick skillet should be heated to medium-high heat. Heat 1 tbsp of the olive oil until shimmering. Place half of the chicken in a single layer in the skillet. Cook the pieces for a further 5 minutes on the other side after flipping them over, until the breading is softly golden brown. Using a slotted spoon, remove the chicken and place it on a plate. Repeat the process with the remaining chicken pieces, including more olive oil as necessary.
4. Melt the butter in the skillet while scraping up any browned bits. The melted butter should be mixed with the buffalo sauces after being added.
5. Buffalo sauce should now include the cooked chicken. After tossing to evenly coat every piece in sauce, simmer the chicken for a further 3 to 5 minutes, or until it is done and the sauce has slightly thickened. Serve right away with split carrots and celery and a blue cheese or ranch dipping sauce.

27. CANDIED PECANS

Prep Time: 10 mins

Cook Time: 40 mins

Total Time: 50 mins

Servings: 10

Ingredients

- ⅓ cup of white sugar, or more as need
- 1 tsp ground cinnamon
- ¼ tsp salt, or more as need
- 1 large egg white
- 1 tbsp water
- 1 pound pecan halves

Directions

1. Set the oven to 250 degrees Fahrenheit (120 degrees C).
2. In a small bowl, mix salt, sugar, and cinnamon.
3. In a big bowl, mix egg white and water and whisk until foamy. Pecans should be coated with the egg white mixture. Pour the sugar mixture in gradually and stir until the pecans are thoroughly covered. Onto a baking sheet, spread.
4. For 10 minutes, bake in the preheated oven. Pecans are stirred and then rearranged in a single layer. Cook the nuts for a further 30 to 50 minutes, stirring every 10 to 15 minutes, until they are evenly browned.

28. VANILLA MANGO SMOOTHIE

Prep Time: 5 minutes

Cook Time: 0 minutes

Total Time: 5 minutes

INGREDIENTS

- 1 cup of refrigerated mango
- 1 refrigerated banana
- 1/2 cup of unsweetened vanilla almond milk*
- 1/2 tsp vanilla extract
- 1 scoop vanilla protein powder (I use North Cost Naturals Vanilla Whey
- non-compulsory: 1 cup of baby spinach

INSTRUCTIONS

1. Blend every item in the blender until it is smooth.
2. Drink right away.
3. Use any non-dairy milk you like. In this smoothie, I adore using unsweetened coconut milk!

29. CHEDDAR CRISPS

Prep2 MIN

Total15 MIN

Servings16

Ingredients

- 1cup of sharp cheddar cheese
- Cayenne pepper

Instructions

1. Set the oven to 425 F. Cooking oil should be sprayed onto a baking pan before adding parchment paper.

2. Spread out every mound of cheddar cheese into an even layer after adding it in mounds of 1 tbsp every. Additionally, provide a space of roughly 1 inch between every cheese round. Add a small amount of cayenne pepper (but not too much) to the dish.

3. Bake for 6 to 10 minutes while keeping an eye on it. The cheese should soften and almost cease bubbling. However, DO NOT let it brown since it will taste harsh.

4. Place on a platter after being removed from the baking sheet. Serve.

30. CHEESE AND ONION DIP

Prep Time15 mins

Total Time15 mins

Servings12 servings

Ingredients

- 1/4 tsp garlic powder
- 1/4 tsp ground black pepper
- 1/2 cup of mayonnaise
- 1/2 cup of sour cream
- 8 ounces cream cheese, softened

- 3 cups of cheddar cheese, shredded
- 1/2 cup of green onions, thinly split

Instructions

1. You should airate your cream cheese before using it, regardless of whether it is spreadable, whipped, in a block, or brick-style. Cream cheese should be moved to a mixing bowl and smoothed out using a mixer. No lumps should exist!

2. The mayonnaise and sour cream should then be added. Smoothly incorporate those into the cream cheese.

3. Garlic powder and black pepper should also be added. To incorporate, stir into the dip.

4. Add the green onions and the crumbled cheddar cheese last. Fold the cheese and green onions in with a spatula or a wooden spoon. To fully integrate all components, thoroughly mix.

5. Refrigerate for two to three hours after transferring to a food-safe container. This will enable the flavors of the components to meld together.

6. Remove from refrigerator and allow it settle at room temperature for 15 to 20 minutes before serving.

Nutrition

1. Calories: 265kcal; Carbohydrates: 3, Protein: 8, Fat: 25, Saturated Fat: 11, Polyunsaturated Fat: 5, Monounsaturated Fat: 6, Trans Fat: 0, Cholesterol: 57, Sodium: 307, Potassium: 73, Fiber: 0, Sugar: 1, Calcium: 232, Iron: 0.2; Carbohydrates: 3, Protein: 8, Fat: 25, Saturated Fat: 11, Polyunsaturated Fat: 5, Trans

31. CHEESY PITA CRISPS

Ready In: 25mins

INGREDIENTS

- 2 whole wheat pita bread
- 1/4 cup of reduced fat margarine
- 1/2 tsp garlic powder
- 1/2 tsp onion powder
- 1/4 tsp salt
- 1/4 tsp pepper
- 3 tbsp parmesan cheese, grated
- 1/2 cup of part-skim mozzarella cheese, grated

DIRECTIONS

2. Divide every pita into two rounds to create four rounds of bread.
3. You will have 16 triangles overall if you slice every circle into 4 triangles.
4. Place every triangle on a baking sheet that has been lightly oiled or sprayed.
5. Spread the remaining ingredients—all but the mozzarella—together over the triangles.
6. Add a little mozzarella.
7. Bake for 12 to 15 minutes, or until golden brown, at 400 degrees.
8. Watch them closely to prevent burning.

32. CHEWY GRANOLA BARS

Prep Time: 10 mins

Cook Time: 20 mins

Additional Time: 10 mins

Total Time: 40 mins

Servings: 18

Ingredients

- 4 ½ cups of rolled oats
- 1 cup of all-purpose flour
- ⅔ cup of butter, softened
- ½ cup of honey
- ⅓ cup of packed brown sugar
- 1 tsp baking soda
- 1 tsp vanilla extract
- 2 cups of miniature semisweet chocolate chips

Directions

1. Set the oven to 325 degrees Fahrenheit (165 degrees C). Grease a 9x13-inch pan sparingly.
2. In a sizable basin, mix the oats, flour, butter, honey, brown sugar, baking soda, and vanilla. Add the chocolate chunks and mix thoroughly. Into the prepared pan, lightly press the oat mixture.
3. Bake for 18 to 22 minutes in a preheated oven, or until golden brown. Slice into bars after let it cool in the pan for 10 minutes. Before removing or serving the bars, let them cool completely in the pan.

33. CHILI LIME TORTILLA CHIPS

Servings 4

Prep Time 15 minutes

Cook Time 30 minutes

Ingredients

- 12 (6-inch) corn tortillas
- 2 tsp chili powder
- 2 tsp from True Lime shaker (or 2 packets of True Lime)
- 2 tsp fine sea salt
- Cooking spray

Directions

1. Oven should be heated to 300 degrees.
2. Slice the tortillas into eighths after stacking them. Onto a baking sheet, transfer.
3. Salt, True Lime, and chili powder should all be mixd in a small bowl. Cooking spray should be briefly misted over the chips before adding the seasonings.
4. *
5. Ensure that the chips are distributed equally on the cookie sheet (you may need more than one, or to make in batches).
6. Bake for 30 to 35 minutes, turning the baking sheet once or twice, or until crisp and golden.

34. CHOCOLATE CHIP BLONDIES

prep time: 10 minutes

cook time: 35 minutes

total time: 45 minutes

Ingredients

- 2 cups of all-purpose flour
- ½ tsp baking powder
- 1 tsp kosher salt

- 2/3 cup of unsalted butter, melted and cooled
- 1 ¾ cups of packed light brown sugar
- 2 large eggs
- 2 tsp pure vanilla extract
- 1 1/2 cups of semisweet chocolate chips
- flakey sea salt, non-compulsory
- Hands Free Mode:
- Prevent screen from sleeping

Instructions

1. Set oven to 350 degrees Fahrenheit. Spray non-stick cooking spray on foil or parchment paper before lining a 9x9-inch baking pan.
2. Mix the flour, baking soda, and salt in a medium bowl.
3. Butter and brown sugar are whisked together in a sizable bowl. Mix in the eggs and vanilla after adding them. Add the dry ingredients gradually and blend just enough. Add chocolate chunks and stir.
4. Pour the batter into the pan as it is ready. Bake in a preheated oven for 35 to 38 minutes, or until a toothpick inserted in the center comes out clean. If wanted, sprinkle some flaky sea salt on top right away. Before sliceting, remove pan to a wire rack and allow cool fully.

35. APPLE CHIPS

PREP TIME: 5 mins

TOTAL TIME: 3 hrs

Ingredients

- 2 apples, thinly split
- 2 tsp. granulated sugar
- 1/2 tsp. cinnamon

Directions

1. ADD TO MY OVEN RECIPES
2. Step 1: 200° oven preheating. Apples should be mixed with sugar and cinnamon in a big basin.
3. Step 2 Set a metal rack inside a baking sheet with a rim. Split apples should not overlap as you place them on the rack's top.
4. Step 3 Bake the apples for two to three hours, turning them over halfway through, until they are dried out but still flexible. (While cooling, apples will continue to crisp.)
5. BY AIR FRYER
6. Step 1 Toss the apples with the sugar and cinnamon in a large bowl. Apples should be placed in a single layer in the air fryer basket as you work in batches (some overlap is okay).
7. Step 2 Bake for approximately 12 minutes at 350°, flipping after 4 minutes.

36. APPLE CINNAMON POPCORN

Prep Time: 5 mins

Total Time: 5 mins

Ingredients

- 4-6 cups of plain popcorn popped
- 2 tbsp coconut oil or unsalted butter
- 1 tbsp honey
- 1/2 tsp vanilla

- 1 tsp Cinnamon or apple pie spice
- 1 cup of apple chips (dehydrated apples pieces)

Instructions

1. Melt coconut oil, unsalted butter, honey, vanilla, cinnamon, or apple pie spice in a small bowl. Mix by whisking.
2. With popped, unflavored popcorn, drizzle and toss.
3. Toss in apple chips with the mixture. Enjoy!
4. Describe your experience if you've tried this dish in the comments section.

5. Nutrition

6. 174 kcal, 28 g carbohydrate, 2 g protein, 8 g fat, 6 g saturated fat, 20 mg sodium, 133 mg potassium, 4 g fiber, 17 g sugar, 1 mg calcium, 8 mg calcium, and 1 mg iron.

37. ALMOND CRANBERRY GRANOLA BARS

Total Time: 50 minutes

INGREDIENTS

- ⅓ cup of maple syrup (or honey)
- 3 tbsp butter, unsalted
- 2 tbsp smooth peanut butter
- 2 tbsp brown sugar, packed
- ½ tsp pure vanilla extract

- ⅛ tsp salt
- 1 ½ cups of old-fashioned rolled oats
- ¾ cup of split almonds
- ⅓ cup of dried cranberries
- ¼ cup of chocolate chips

INSTRUCTIONS

1. Set the oven to 325 F.
2. Mix maple syrup, butter, peanut butter, brown sugar, vanilla, and salt in a medium pot. Stirring continuously, heat over medium-low heat until butter melts and sugar dissolves.
3. Almonds and oats should be mixd in a medium mixing basin. The warm liquid mixture should be poured over the oats and mixd. Give the mixture 10 minutes to reach room temperature. As a result, the chocolate won't melt when mixd. If you lack the patience to wait for the mixture to cool, you can still add the chocolate chips, but be aware that they will melt into the batter and lose their exquisite flavor.
4. Add the chocolate chips and cranberries and stir.
5. Place the mixture in a 9-inch square baking pan or casserole that has been lined with parchment paper. Make use of a spatula or the back of a glass to firmly push the mixture into the pan. Make sure it is securely packed if possible.
6. 20 to 25 minutes of baking (or add more time for crunchier granola bars).
7. For at least two hours, let the food totally cool in the fridge. After that, slice into bars and serve.

38. CREAMY SPINACH CRAB DIP

TOTAL TIME 60minutes

SERVINGS 12servings

INGREDIENTS

- 1 (6 oz) can Chicken of the Sea® Lump Crab, drained
- 3 cloves garlic, chop up
- 1 Tbsp butter
- 2 cups of fresh baby spinach, coarsely chop up
- 8 oz. cream cheese, softened
- 1/2 cup of mayonnaise
- 1/2 cup of shredded Parmesan cheese
- 1/4 tsp cayenne pepper
- 1 tsp salt, or as need
- 1 tsp black pepper, or as need
- Fresh baguette, crackers or endives, for dipping

INSTRUCTIONS

1. Set the oven to 400 °F.
2. Butter should be used to sauté garlic until just golden. Add the spinach and cook it until it wilts. Place aside.
3. Cream cheese, mayonnaise, Parmesan cheese, cayenne, salt, and pepper should all be thoroughly mixd in a big basin.
4. Add crab and spinach to the cheese mixture. Stir everything together.
5. To a medium baking dish, transfer.
6. After 40 minutes of baking, broil for 2-4 minutes to brown the top.
7. Serve with fresh baguette and crackers. Serve with veggies or endive leaves for choices that are gluten-free or low in carbs.

39. CHEDDAR CHEESE PUFFS

PREP TIME 5 mins

COOK TIME 45 mins

TOTAL TIME 50 mins

SERVINGS 24 servings

Ingredients

- 1 stick butter (8 tbsp or 4 ounces)
- 1 cup of water
- 1/2 tsp salt
- 1 cup of all-purpose flour
- 4 large eggs
- 1 cup of (4 ounces) grated sharp cheddar cheese
- 2 tsp chop up fresh thyme or rosemary
- Freshly ground pepper

Method

1. Salt, butter, and water to boil: Mix the salt, butter, and water in a medium saucepan and heat to a rolling boil.

2. Reduce the heat to medium, then slowly add the flour while stirring. Stirring quickly A dough ball will be formed from the mixture, and it will start to pull away from the pan's sides.

3. The dough will be quite thick, so it helps to stir with a wooden spoon. Cooking should continue for a few minutes.

4. Allow it cool for a few minutes before adding eggs one at a time:

5. After taking the pan from the heat, give it a few moments to cool. Stirring will help the dough cool more uniformly. The dough should be warm, but not so hot that the eggs begin to cook as soon as they contact the dough.

6. One at a time, add the eggs and toss the dough after every addition to incorporate the eggs. (You can use a mixer for this step, or you can do it by hand with a wooden spoon.) The dough ought to start to get fairly creamy.

7. Add some peppercorns, thyme, and cheese that has been grated.

8. Scoop spoonfuls onto a lined baking sheet:

9. 425°F oven temperature. On a silicone or parchment-lined baking sheet, drop small balls of dough (approximately a heaping tbsp) with at least an inch between every one.

10. Bake for 10 minutes at 425 degrees Fahrenheit. Reduce heat to 350°F and continue to cook for an additional 15 to 20 minutes, or until puffy and gently brown.

40. APPLE FRIES

Total: 45 min

Active: 45 min

Ingredients

- Vegetable oil, for frying
- 4 Granny Smith apples, peel off

- 1/2 cup of cornstarch
- 1/2 cup of + 2 tbsp granulated sugar
- 1 tsp ground cinnamon
- 2/3 cup of heavy cream
- 1 tsp pure vanilla extract

Directions

1. In a large, wide saucepan, heat 1 1/2 inches of vegetable oil over medium heat until a deep-fry thermometer reads 300 degrees F. To make the apples look like fries, slice them into 1/2-inch-wide sticks.

2. Shake off any extra cornstarch after thoroughly coating the apples in two batches. Fry for 2 minutes or until softened but still pale in the heated oil. Remove with a slotted spoon and transfer in a single layer to a rack placed over a rimmed baking sheet to cool. Between batches, allow the oil to warm back up to 300 degrees F.

3. In a small bowl, mix 1/2 cup of sugar and the cinnamon; reserve. In a medium bowl, use an electric mixer to whip the heavy cream, vanilla, and last 2 tbsp of sugar into medium peaks.

4. Heat the oil to 375 degrees Fahrenheit. Re-fry the apples for 1 1/2 minutes, working in about three batches, until crisp and lightly browned. After briefly draining on paper towels, remove the food and stir in the cinnamon sugar until thoroughly coated. Serve hot with whipped cream on the side for dipping.

41. DOUBLE CHOCOLATE BISCOTTI

Prep Time: 20 Minutes

Cook Time: 50 Minutes

Total Time: 1 Hour 10 Minutes

INGREDIENTS

- 1¾ cups of + 2 tbsp all-purpose flour, spooned into measuring cup of and leveled-off
- ¼ cup of + 2 tbsp natural unsweetened cocoa powder, such as Hershey's

- 1 tsp baking soda
- ¾ tsp salt
- 1 stick (8 tbsp) unsalted butter, at room temperature
- ¾ cup of + 2 tbsp granulated sugar
- 2 large eggs
- 2 tsp vanilla extract
- 1 cup of semi-sweet chocolate chips

INSTRUCTIONS

1. A baking sheet should be lined with parchment paper and the oven should be preheated to 350°F.
2. Mix the flour, cocoa powder, baking soda, and salt in a medium basin.
3. Cream the butter and sugar in the bowl of an electric mixer for one to two minutes, or until they are light and fluffy. Apply a rubber spatula to the bowl's sides to scrape them down. One at a time, add the eggs, scraping the bowl between additions and thoroughly combining every one. the vanilla afterward. On low speed, add the dry ingredients and chocolate chips, and whisk just until blended.
4. Add flour to the work surface. Scrape the sticky dough onto the work surface with a rubber spatula, then sprinkle a little flour over the top. To slice the dough in half, form a rough ball with your hands. If the dough is still too sticky, add a little more flour. Roll the dough pieces back and forth to form two short logs. Shape the logs into longer logs that are approximately 34 inch high and 2 inches wide before placing them onto the prepared baking sheet. Give the logs ample room to stretch out a bit while baking. Bake for approximately 35 minutes, or until touchably hard. If you wait much longer, the biscotti won't be easy to slice; instead, let the biscotti logs cool on the pan for approximately 5 minutes, or until they are just cool enough to touch. Then, using a sharp knife, slice the logs into 34-inch slices on the diagonal (I do this right on the baking sheet). They will break slightly; don't be concerned. The biscotti should be placed back in the oven for 10 minutes to dry and crisp up. Flip the biscotti over so that the slice sides are facing up. After a few minutes of cooling on the pan, remove to a wire rack to finish cooling. Serve with warm milk, coffee, or tea.
5. Freezer-Friendly Instructions: Up to three months of freezing is possible for the dough: The dough should be formed into logs, every wrapped tightly in plastic wrap, and put in a bag that can be sealed. When you're ready to bake, take the logs out of the freezer, let the dough thaw until workable, and then follow the recipe. Once baking, cookies can be refrigerated by double-wrapping them in freezer wrap or aluminum foil after they have completely cooled. Before serving, let the food thaw overnight on the counter.

42. FIG BARS

Prep 30 Min

Total 1 Hr 50 Min

Servings 16

Ingredients

- Crust
- 1/2 cup of butter or margarine, softened
- 1/4 cup of granulated sugar
- 1/4 tsp vanilla
- 1 cup of Gold Medal™ all-purpose flour
- Filling
- 1/4 cup of granulated sugar
- 1 cup of boiling water
- 1 bag (9 oz) dried Mission figs, chop up (1 cup of)
- Topping
- 1/4 cup of Gold Medal™ all-purpose flour
- 1/4 cup of packed brown sugar
- 3 tbsp cold butter (do not use margarine)
- 1/4 cup of quick-cooking oats
- 1/4 cup of chop up walnuts

Steps

1. 350°F oven temperature. Spray cooking spray in a 9-inch square pan. Using an electric mixer set to medium speed, thoroughly mix 1/2 cup of butter, 1/4 cup of granulated sugar, and the vanilla in a small dish. Beat in 1 cup of flour at a low speed until a soft dough forms. In the pan's bottom, press the dough. Until the middle is firm, bake for 10 to 15 minutes.

2. In the meantime, boil the filling ingredients in a 2-quart saucepan over medium-high heat for 5 to 10 minutes, stirring often, or until the figs are soft and most of the liquid has been absorbed. over the crust.

3. Using a pastry cutter or fork, mix 1/4 cup of flour, the brown sugar, and 3 tbsp butter in a small bowl until crumbly. Add walnuts and oats and stir. Dot over the filling.

4. Bake for an additional 15 to 20 minutes, or until topping is lightly golden brown and edges are bubbling. About an hour to totally cool. Slice the bars into four rows by four rows.

43. THE BEST LEMON BARS

Prep Time: 15 mins

Cook Time: 35 mins

Total Time: 50 mins

Servings: 24

Ingredients

- Crust:
- 2 cups of all-purpose flour
- 1 cup of butter, softened
- ½ cup of white sugar

- Filling:
- 1 ½ cups of white sugar
- ¼ cup of all-purpose flour
- 4 eggs
- 2 lemons, juiced

Directions

1. Set the oven to 350 degrees Fahrenheit (175 degrees C).
2. Making the crust In a medium bowl, stir together 2 cups of flour, 1/2 cup of sugar, and softened butter. Press into the bottom of a 9x13-inch pan that has not been oiled.
3. Bake for about 15 minutes, or until firm and brown in the preheated oven. Make the filling in the interim: In a larger basin, mix 1/4 cup of flour and the remaining 1 1/2 cups of sugar. When the mixture is smooth, whisk in the eggs and lemon juice. Then, pour it over the baking crust.
4. For 20 minutes, bake in the preheated oven. The bars will firm up as they cool, so set the pan aside to completely cool. Slice the cooled cake into even squares.

44. FREEZER FUDGE

Prep Time 10 minutes

Cook Time 0 minutes

Freezing time 4 hours

Total Time 4 hours 10 minutes

Servings 16

Ingredients

- 1 cup of smooth peanut butter (with no added sugar or salt)
- 1/2 cup of maple syrup
- 1/4 cup of unsweetened cocoa powder
- 1 tsp pure vanilla extract
- 1/8 tsp salt

Instructions

1. *In a mixing dish, mix the peanut butter, maple syrup, unsweetened cocoa powder, vanilla extract, and salt.*
2. *If you don't want your hands to get sticky, wear cooking gloves and mix with your hands until the mixture is thick and resembles cookie dough.*
3. *Transfer to a medium loaf pan that has been lined with parchment paper (my loaf pan is 9.25 x 5.25 x 2.75 inches).*
4. *Press the fudge into an equal layer using your hands.*
5. *Before serving or storing the fudge squares in the freezer, freeze for at least four hours before sliceting into squares.*

Notes

1. 1/4 cup of chop up peanuts, walnuts, or pecans are non-compulsory additions (mixed into the fudge before transferring it to the loaf pan).
2. Store this freezer fudge in an airtight container in the freezer for up to six months.

Made in United States
Troutdale, OR
04/14/2025